Knowledge of SELF (Social Empowerment Learning Framework)

Young Adult Edition (Ages 18–21)

TM

Student Workbook

Written by Cedric A. Washington

Table of Contents

Table of Contents... Continued.

™

Knowledge
of S.E.L.F.
Curriculum

Knowledge of SELF Curriculum — Middle School Student Workbook

© 2025 by Cedric A. Washington

For permission requests, write to the publisher at the address below.

Who Lives Like This?! Publishing LLC
www.nerdyouthservices.org

ISBN: 978-1-970680-14-0 (Paperback)

Cover design and interior layout by
Who Lives Like This?! Publishing LLC Design Team

Printed in the United States of America

First Edition — 2025

About the Author

Cedric A. Washington is a master educator, speaker, author, former college basketball player, and the Executive Director of NERD Youth Services, Inc. A native of Gary, Indiana. Over two decades of experience in education, mentoring, and community leadership have fueled his commitment to building culturally responsive, empowering programs for African American youth. As the visionary behind the Knowledge of SELF (Social Empowerment Learning Framework) curriculum, Cedric blends historical awareness, emotional intelligence, leadership training, and personal reflection to cultivate greatness in every student he reaches. His work has been celebrated nationally at education conferences, faith institutions, and youth leadership summits. Cedric's mission is simple but powerful: To equip young people with the self-knowledge, discipline, and purpose they need to transform themselves — and the world.

Daily Affirmations

I AM a trailblazer. I AM destined to succeed. Speak it. Believe it. Do it. – Cedric A. Washington

- I am enough, just as I am.
- My history is powerful, my future is greater.
- I am not what the world calls me—I am who God created me to be.
- I will lead with love, courage, and clarity.
- My skin, my hair, my mind—divinely designed.
- I rise above every label and lie.
- Greatness is not ahead of me; it's within me.
- I walk in wisdom and purpose.
- I am part of a legacy of excellence.
- I build, I uplift, I transform.

Pre-Reflection Survey

Before starting the Knowledge of SELF curriculum, please answer honestly:

1. What do you currently know about your cultural identity?

2. How confident are you in making positive decisions for your future? (1–5)

3. What does success mean to you?

4. Have you ever felt misunderstood in school or in life? Explain.

5. What do you hope to gain from this experience?

Knowledge of SELF (Social Empowerment Learning Framework) Young Adult Edition (Ages 18–21) — Student Workbook

Unit One: SELF Conscience

Lesson 1: Am I a Color? (Part 1)

Objective:
Students will critically examine the historical evolution of racial identity labels and their impact on self-perception.

Do Now:
Do you identify yourself as African American? What does that mean to you?

_____
_____
_____
_____
_____
_____
_____
_____
_____
_____

Mini-Lesson:
- Terms like Negro, Colored, Black, Afro American, and African American were historically assigned.
- Ethnicity vs. Nationality: Understand the difference and why it matters.

Activity:
Historical Reflection:
- Analyze the terms historically used for our people.
- Research and discuss the origins of these labels.

Critical Thinking Questions:
1. How have labels shaped how we see ourselves and how others see us?

_____
_____
_____
_____
_____
_____

_____
_____
_____

2. Can a person truly know themselves if they don't understand the history behind their identity?

_____
_____
_____
_____
_____
_____
_____
_____
_____
_____

Journal Prompt:
What does reclaiming your true identity mean to you?
[Write two full paragraphs.]

_____
_____
_____
_____
_____
_____
_____
_____
_____
_____
_____
_____
_____
_____
_____
_____

Lesson 2: Am I a Color? (Part 2)

Objective:
Students will deepen understanding of historical identity through biblical references and cultural reflection.

Do Now:
What is the purpose of school? What is the purpose of church?

_____
_____
_____
_____
_____
_____
_____
_____
_____
_____
_____

Mini-Lesson:
- Pre-slavery history exists, but has been hidden — largely located in biblical text (Genesis, Exodus, Deuteronomy, Revelation).
- Academic history often starts with slavery — omitting our true beginning.

Activity:
Scriptural Study and Identity:
- Explore Deuteronomy Chapter 28 and discuss curses, prophecy, and identity.

Critical Thinking Questions:
1. Why is it important to question where history "starts" in school textbooks?

_____
_____
_____
_____
_____
_____
_____
_____
_____
_____

2. How does biblical history strengthen or challenge what you thought about your identity?

_____
_____
_____
_____
_____
_____
_____
_____
_____
_____

Journal Prompt:
What emotions did you experience learning this information? How does it reshape your thinking?
[Write two full paragraphs.]

_____
_____
_____
_____
_____
_____
_____
_____
_____
_____
_____
_____
_____
_____
_____
_____
_____
_____
_____

Lesson 3: Love Yourself — The Skin You're In

Objective:
Students will embrace their unique skin tones, understand melanin's power, and critically analyze the use of color labels.

Do Now:
How do you feel about your skin tone today?

_____
_____
_____
_____
_____
_____
_____
_____
_____
_____
_____

Mini-Lesson:
- Melanin is a biological blessing, not a burden.
- Melanin: 6 protons, 6 neutrons, 6 electrons — the original 666 (power, not curse).

Activity:
Skin Tone Matching:
- Students use a Skin Tone Chart to identify their natural shade — realizing none are truly "black" or "white."

"I don't want to be in the sun too long because I don't want to get black." **How many times have we either heard or said this comment? The very thing that we don't want to get is the sole source of our dominance, melanin. Melanin is made up of 6 protons, 6 neutrons, and 6 electrons, 666. When the numbers 666 are often mentioned it's referred by mainstream media as the mark of the beast.**

However, when you gain knowledge of SELF, one begins to learn that the so called African American or black people aren't even the color that they sing loud and proud about. Look at the Skin Tone Chart and match your skin complexion with the shades of brown on the Skin Tone Chart.

Color Me Human | Skin Tone Chart   expl◯ratorium

A1 B1 C1 D1 E1 F1
A2 B2 C2 D2 E2 F2
A3 B3 C3 D3 E3 F3
A4 B4 C4 D4 E4 F4
A5 B5 C5 D5 E5 F5
A6 B6 C6 D6 E6 F6
A7 B7 C7 D7 E7 F7
A8 B8 C8 D8 E8 F8
A9 B9 C9 D9 E9 F9
A10 B10 C10 D10 E10 F10
A11 B11 C11 D11 E11 F11

Critical **Thinking time**:
We talk about the power of words, so let's discuss the two terms we use to describe people, black and white.

Have students go to Merriam Webster to define the terms black and white. Discuss with students the difference of the two terms and why if we say there are power in words, why do we identify ourselves with such a negative word? Why is the term white described positive? How do you feel about the information you learned today? Do you feel empowered?

Critical Thinking Questions:
1. Why are we taught color labels that distort our natural beauty?

_____
_____
_____
_____
_____
_____
_____
_____
_____
_____
_____
_____

2. How can understanding your biology change your self-esteem?

_____
_____
_____
_____
_____
_____
_____
_____
_____
_____

Journal Prompt:
What is the power of loving your authentic self, skin and soul?
[Write two full paragraphs.]

_____
_____
_____
_____
_____
_____
_____
_____
_____
_____
_____
_____
_____
_____
_____
_____
_____
_____

Lesson 4: Attributes/Characteristics of SELF

Objective:
Students will reflect on their unique attributes and character traits to build self-awareness and purpose.

Do Now:
What three words would you want someone to use to describe you?

_____
_____
_____
_____
_____
_____
_____
_____
_____
_____
_____

Mini-Lesson:
- Self-conscience requires honest reflection about your strengths and areas for growth.
- True power comes from knowing your own blueprint.

Activity:
Attribute Discovery:
- List 5 personal strengths and 2 areas you want to improve.

Critical Thinking Questions:
1. How does understanding your characteristics shape your goals?

_____
_____
_____
_____
_____
_____
_____

2. Why is being honest about your strengths and weaknesses important for leadership?

_____
_____
_____
_____
_____
_____
_____
_____
_____
_____

Journal Prompt:
If you could add one new powerful trait to your character, what would it be and why?
[Write two full paragraphs.]

_____
_____
_____
_____
_____
_____
_____
_____
_____
_____
_____
_____
_____
_____
_____
_____
_____
_____
_____
_____
_____

Lesson 5: Ethics

Objective:
Students will define their personal code of ethics and understand how it impacts every decision they make.

Do Now:
Name one decision you're proud of because you stood on your principles.

_____
_____
_____
_____
_____
_____
_____
_____
_____
_____
_____

Mini-Lesson:
- Ethics are personal laws you live by even when no one is watching.
- Without ethics, greatness collapses.

Activity:
Ethical Compass:
- List your Top 5 values and write how they guide your life choices.

Critical Thinking Questions:
1. How does having strong ethics protect your future?

_____
_____
_____
_____
_____
_____
_____
_____
_____
_____
_____

2. Why must your actions match your words if you want lasting respect?

_____
_____
_____
_____
_____
_____
_____
_____
_____
_____

Journal Prompt:
What is one ethical standard you refuse to compromise on?
[Write two full paragraphs.]

_____
_____
_____
_____
_____
_____
_____
_____
_____
_____
_____
_____
_____
_____
_____
_____
_____
_____

Lesson 6: Image

Objective:
Students will explore the difference between public image and private reality, and commit to authenticity.

Do Now:
What's one thing about yourself you wish the world knew without you having to say it?

_____
_____
_____
_____
_____
_____
_____
_____
_____
_____
_____
_____

Mini-Lesson:
- Public image is what people see. Private image is who you really are.
- Power is when both align.

Activity:
Mirror Exercise:
- Write 5 things the world thinks about you and 5 things you know about yourself.
- Reflect on the differences.

Critical Thinking Questions:
1. How does public image influence opportunity and trust?

_____
_____
_____
_____
_____
_____
_____
_____
_____
_____
_____

2. Why is being true to yourself even more important than being liked?

_____
_____
_____
_____
_____
_____
_____
_____
_____
_____

Journal Prompt:
How will you build an image that is authentic, strong, and lasting?
[Write two full paragraphs.]

_____
_____
_____
_____
_____
_____
_____
_____
_____
_____
_____
_____
_____
_____
_____
_____
_____
_____
_____

Lesson 7: Achievements

Objective:
Students will identify personal achievements, build pride in growth, and set vision for future accomplishments.

Do Now:
What achievement are you most proud of so far?

_____
_____
_____
_____
_____
_____
_____
_____
_____
_____
_____
_____

Mini-Lesson:
- Celebrate your wins — even small ones.
- Achievements are stepping stones, not finish lines.

Activity:
Victory Reflection:
- List your top 5 achievements so far (small or large).
- Write 1 future achievement goal for the next year.

Critical Thinking Questions:
1. How does celebrating your achievements fuel your confidence for the next level?

_____
_____
_____
_____
_____
_____
_____
_____
_____
_____
_____

2. Why must we recognize growth instead of only chasing perfection?

_____
_____
_____
_____
_____
_____
_____
_____
_____
_____

Journal Prompt:
Describe a future achievement you can see yourself celebrating — and what it will mean to you.
[Write two full paragraphs.]

_____
_____
_____
_____
_____
_____
_____
_____
_____
_____
_____
_____
_____
_____
_____
_____
_____
_____
_____
_____
_____

Knowledge of SELF (Social Empowerment Learning Framework) Young Adult Edition (Ages 18–21) — Student Workbook

Unit Two: SELF Governing

Lesson 1: Health and Nutrition

Objective:
Students will understand the importance of physical health and nutrition as foundations for personal and professional success.

Do Now:
What is one healthy habit you practice or would like to start?

_____

_____

_____

_____

_____

_____

_____

_____

_____

_____

Mini-Lesson:
- Your body is your first vehicle for greatness — fuel it accordingly.
- Sea moss, water intake, exercise, and rest are non-negotiables for warriors.

Activity:
Health Master Plan:
- List 3 small changes you can make to your eating or physical activity this week.

Critical Thinking Questions:
1. How does health impact not just your body but your mindset and energy?

_____

_____

_____

_____

_____

_____

_____

_____

_____

_____

_____

_____

2. Why is mastering your health the first sign of mastering your life?

_____
_____
_____
_____
_____
_____
_____
_____
_____
_____
_____
_____

Journal Prompt:
What would your "Healthy SELF" look and feel like? How will you build it?
[Write two full paragraphs.]

_____
_____
_____
_____
_____
_____
_____
_____
_____
_____
_____
_____
_____
_____
_____

Lesson 2: The Importance of FOCUS

Objective:
Students will internalize F.O.C.U.S. as a personal system for achieving goals.

Do Now:
Why do you think staying focused is so difficult in today's world?

_____
_____
_____
_____
_____
_____
_____
_____
_____
_____
_____
_____

Mini-Lesson:
- F.O.C.U.S.: Fallback, Opportunities, Cultivate, Understanding, Succeed.
- True focus isn't random — it's a chosen lifestyle.

Activity:
FOCUS Reflection:
- Write what each letter in F.O.C.U.S. personally means to you.
- Create a "Focus Map" for one goal you want to achieve.

Critical Thinking Questions:
1. Why is it necessary to fallback from distractions to rise into purpose?

_____
_____
_____
_____
_____
_____
_____
_____
_____
_____

2. How does understanding that everyone won't understand empower you to succeed?

_____
_____
_____
_____
_____
_____
_____
_____
_____
_____
_____

Journal Prompt:
What will you sacrifice today so you can succeed tomorrow?
[Write two full paragraphs.]

_____
_____
_____
_____
_____
_____
_____
_____
_____
_____
_____
_____
_____
_____
_____
_____
_____
_____
_____

Lesson 3: Attributes/Characteristics of SELF

Objective:
Students will define the impact of role modeling and commit to being a positive influence.

Do Now:
Who is one person you look up to? What qualities inspire you?

_____
_____
_____
_____
_____
_____
_____
_____
_____
_____

Mini-Lesson:
- You are a living, breathing example — whether you realize it or not.
- Someone younger is always watching.

Activity:
Legacy Leadership:
- List 5 traits you want to model for others.

Critical Thinking Questions:
1. Why is it powerful to consciously live as someone else's inspiration?

_____
_____
_____
_____
_____
_____
_____
_____
_____
_____
_____
_____

2. How does being a positive role model make you better too?

_____
_____
_____
_____
_____
_____
_____
_____
_____
_____
_____
_____

Journal Prompt:
What kind of role model will you be for your family, community, and future?
[Write two full paragraphs.]

_____
_____
_____
_____
_____
_____
_____
_____
_____
_____
_____
_____
_____
_____
_____
_____
_____

Lesson 4: Hygiene

Objective:
Students will understand the importance of personal hygiene for health, confidence, and respect.

Do Now:
Why is hygiene important for how you feel and how others perceive you?

_____
_____
_____
_____
_____
_____
_____
_____
_____
_____
_____
_____

Mini-Lesson:
- Hygiene is self-respect made visible.
- Small habits today protect your future health and opportunities.

Activity:
Hygiene Check List:
- List daily hygiene habits that build confidence and protect health.

Critical Thinking Questions:
1. How does maintaining hygiene impact your self-esteem and opportunities?

_____
_____
_____
_____
_____
_____
_____
_____
_____
_____

2. Why is daily discipline in hygiene a reflection of your personal standards?

_____
_____
_____
_____
_____
_____
_____
_____
_____
_____
_____
_____
_____

Journal Prompt:
What hygiene habit are you committed to mastering?
[Write two full paragraphs.]

_____
_____
_____
_____
_____
_____
_____
_____
_____
_____
_____
_____
_____
_____
_____
_____
_____

Lesson 5: Emotional Maturity

Objective:
Students will understand emotional maturity as the ability to manage emotions and navigate relationships wisely.

Do Now:
What is one situation where emotional maturity helped you or could have helped you?

_____

_____

_____

_____

_____

_____

_____

_____

_____

_____

_____

Mini-Lesson:
- Emotional maturity is about mastering reaction, not pretending you don't feel.
- It's about responding, not reacting.

Activity:
Maturity Map:
- Identify 3 emotional triggers and plan how to respond maturely.

Critical Thinking Questions:
1. How does emotional maturity give you power in tough situations?

_____

_____

_____

_____

_____

_____

_____

_____

_____

_____

_____

2. Why is emotional discipline more valuable than just physical strength?

_____

_____

_____

_____

_____

_____

_____

_____

_____

_____

_____

_____

_____

Journal Prompt:
Describe one area where you will grow emotionally this year.
[Write two full paragraphs.]

_____

_____

_____

_____

_____

_____

_____

_____

_____

_____

_____

_____

_____

_____

_____

_____

_____

Lesson 6: Puberty and Self-Respect

Objective:
Students will understand puberty changes with an emphasis on self-respect, health, and identity development.

Do Now:
What is one positive or challenging experience you remember about growing through puberty?

_____
_____
_____
_____
_____
_____
_____
_____
_____
_____
_____

Mini-Lesson:
- Puberty is not just physical growth — it's the blueprint for who you're becoming.
- Self-respect is your greatest tool during this stage.

Activity:
Body Awareness Reflection:
- Discuss physical, emotional, and mental changes.
- Create a "Growth Affirmation" celebrating your journey.

Critical Thinking Questions:
1. How does understanding your body help you protect and respect yourself?

_____
_____
_____
_____
_____
_____
_____
_____
_____
_____

2. Why is positive self-talk essential during this time of growth?

_____

_____

_____

_____

_____

_____

_____

_____

_____

_____

_____

_____

Journal Prompt:
What would you tell your younger self about growing up?
[Write two full paragraphs.]

_____

_____

_____

_____

_____

_____

_____

_____

_____

_____

_____

_____

_____

_____

_____

_____

_____

Lesson 7: Peer Pressure

Objective:
Students will identify types of peer pressure and build strategies to stay true to themselves under pressure.

Do Now:
Describe a time when you resisted or gave in to peer pressure. How did you feel?

_____
_____
_____
_____
_____
_____
_____
_____
_____

Mini-Lesson:
- Peer pressure isn't always loud — sometimes it's silent.
- Courage is choosing your path even when others choose differently.

Activity:
Pressure Breakers:
- Identify 3 peer pressure scenarios and create "escape scripts" to resist them.

Critical Thinking Questions:
1. Why is protecting your SELF more important than pleasing your peers?

_____
_____
_____
_____
_____
_____
_____
_____
_____
_____
_____
_____
_____

2. How does walking alone sometimes make you a true leader?

Journal Prompt:
What boundary will you honor even if no one else understands?
[Write two full paragraphs.]

_____
_____
_____
_____
_____
_____
_____
_____
_____
_____
_____
_____
_____
_____
_____
_____
_____
_____
_____
_____
_____
_____
_____

Knowledge of SELF (Social Empowerment Learning Framework)

Young Adult Edition (Ages 18–21) — Student Workbook

Unit Three: Social Conscience

Lesson 1: How to Be Effective in Your Community

Objective:
Students will learn how to become agents of change by contributing meaningfully to their communities.

Do Now:
Name one positive change you'd like to see in your community.

_____
_____
_____
_____
_____
_____
_____
_____
_____
_____
_____
_____

Mini-Lesson:
- Change doesn't require permission — it requires action.
- Start where you are, use what you have, do what you can.

Activity:
Community Action Blueprint:
- Identify a community need and outline 3 ways to contribute or create change.

Critical Thinking Questions:
1. Why is service to your community essential for real leadership?

_____
_____
_____
_____
_____
_____
_____
_____
_____
_____

2. How can small acts of service lead to major social change?

_____
_____
_____
_____
_____
_____
_____
_____
_____
_____
_____
_____

Journal Prompt:
What community need speaks to your heart, and how will you answer the call?
[Write two full paragraphs.]

_____
_____
_____
_____
_____
_____
_____
_____
_____
_____
_____
_____
_____
_____
_____
_____
_____
_____

Lesson 2: African American Leaders

Objective:
Students will study key African American leaders and identify leadership traits to emulate.

Do Now:
Name a Black leader who inspires you. What quality stands out?

_____
_____
_____
_____
_____
_____
_____
_____
_____
_____

Mini-Lesson:
- Leadership is built on vision, courage, and sacrifice.
- Our ancestors planted seeds — it's our job to grow forests.

Activity:
Legacy Leaders Project:
- Choose an African American leader.
- Research their achievements, struggles, and strategies for impact.

Critical Thinking Questions:
1. What leadership qualities do you admire most from historical and modern figures?

_____
_____
_____
_____
_____
_____
_____
_____
_____
_____
_____
_____
_____

2. How does studying leaders help you build your own leadership style?

_____
_____
_____
_____
_____
_____
_____
_____
_____
_____
_____
_____
_____
_____
_____

Journal Prompt:
If a future generation studies your leadership, what would you want them to learn from you?
[Write two full paragraphs.]

_____
_____
_____
_____
_____
_____
_____
_____
_____
_____
_____
_____
_____
_____

Lesson 3: Hip Hop: The Culture

Objective:
Students will explore the roots of Hip Hop as a cultural movement of empowerment, creativity, and resistance.

Do Now:
How has Hip Hop impacted your life or the world around you?

_____
_____
_____
_____
_____
_____
_____
_____
_____

Mini-Lesson:
- Hip Hop was born from struggle, creativity, resistance, and survival.
- It's more than music — it's storytelling, innovation, and liberation.

Activity:
Cultural Impact Analysis:
- Analyze a Hip Hop song or artist who uses their platform to uplift, educate, or inspire.

Critical Thinking Questions:
1. How has Hip Hop been used as a voice for the voiceless?

_____
_____
_____
_____
_____
_____
_____
_____
_____
_____
_____
_____

2. Why is it important to protect the culture's roots and original messages?

_____
_____
_____
_____
_____
_____
_____
_____
_____
_____
_____
_____
_____
_____

Journal Prompt:
If you created a Hip Hop anthem about your life and mission, what would it be called?
[Write two full paragraphs.]

_____
_____
_____
_____
_____
_____
_____
_____
_____
_____
_____
_____
_____
_____
_____
_____
_____
_____
_____

Lesson 4: Family Dynamics

Objective:
Students will explore the structure and influence of family on personal development and community building.

Do Now:
What role does family play in shaping who you are?

_____
_____
_____
_____
_____
_____
_____
_____
_____

Mini-Lesson:
- Families are the first societies — building blocks of culture, strength, and sometimes struggle.
- Healing your family patterns is part of building your legacy.

Activity:
Family Tree Reflection:
- Draw your family tree.
- Highlight 3 values you've inherited and 3 you will improve for future generations.

Critical Thinking Questions:
1. How do family dynamics influence your leadership and life decisions?

_____
_____
_____
_____
_____
_____
_____
_____
_____
_____
_____

2. How can you be a change agent within your own family?

_____
_____
_____
_____
_____
_____
_____
_____
_____
_____
_____
_____

Journal Prompt:
What legacy do you want your family line to carry after you?
[Write two full paragraphs.]

_____
_____
_____
_____
_____
_____
_____
_____
_____
_____
_____
_____
_____
_____
_____

Lesson 5: Accountability

Objective:
Students will learn why personal accountability is the cornerstone of real power and respect.

Do Now:
Think of a time you took full responsibility for something. How did it feel?

_____
_____
_____
_____
_____
_____
_____
_____
_____
_____
_____

Mini-Lesson:
- Accountability is not blame — it's ownership.
- Leaders own their wins and their mistakes.

Activity:
Accountability Reflection:
- Write about a time you succeeded because you took full ownership.

Critical Thinking Questions:
1. Why is accountability necessary for building trust and leadership?

_____
_____
_____
_____
_____
_____
_____
_____
_____
_____
_____
_____
_____

2. How does accountability help you control your destiny?

_____
_____
_____
_____
_____
_____
_____
_____
_____
_____
_____
_____
_____
_____

Journal Prompt:
What area of your life would improve if you stepped up your accountability?
[Write two full paragraphs.]

_____
_____
_____
_____
_____
_____
_____
_____
_____
_____
_____
_____
_____
_____
_____
_____
_____

Lesson 6: Community Service and Giving Back

Objective:
Students will understand the importance of giving back to the community and how service builds legacy.

Do Now:
What is one cause you feel passionate about?

_____
_____
_____
_____
_____
_____
_____

Mini-Lesson:
- Real kings and queens serve their people.
- Your gift is not just for you — it's for others too.

Activity:
Service Planning:
- Plan one service project you could complete this year (food drive, mentorship, clean-up, etc.).

Critical Thinking Questions:
1. How does service strengthen both the giver and the receiver?

_____
_____
_____
_____
_____
_____
_____
_____
_____
_____
_____
_____
_____

2. Why is giving back essential to building a powerful legacy?

_____
_____
_____
_____
_____
_____
_____
_____
_____
_____
_____
_____

Journal Prompt:
What type of community service will you commit to in the next 12 months?
[Write two full paragraphs.]

_____
_____
_____
_____
_____
_____
_____
_____
_____
_____
_____
_____
_____
_____
_____
_____

Lesson 7: Building Your Legacy

Objective:
Students will create a personal blueprint for building a lasting legacy through actions, impact, and leadership.

Do Now:
What is one word you want people to use to describe your life's work?

_____
_____
_____
_____
_____
_____
_____
_____

Mini-Lesson:
- Legacy is not money — it's impact.
- What you build now echoes through time.

Activity:
Legacy Vision Board:
- Create a vision board representing the legacy you want to leave behind.

Critical Thinking Questions:
1. How does thinking about your legacy change the way you live today?

_____
_____
_____
_____
_____
_____
_____
_____
_____
_____
_____

2. Why is it important to live intentionally, not accidentally?

_____

_____

_____

_____

_____

_____

_____

_____

_____

_____

_____

_____

_____

Journal Prompt:
If you could be remembered for one thing, what would it be?
[Write two full paragraphs.]

_____

_____

_____

_____

_____

_____

_____

_____

_____

_____

_____

_____

_____

_____

_____

_____

_____

Knowledge of SELF (Social Empowerment Learning Framework)

Young Adult Edition (Ages 18–21) — Student Workbook

TM

Unit Four: Aspirations

Lesson 1: What I Want to Be When I Grow Up

Objective:
Students will define their aspirations and align their passions with career paths and personal missions.

Do Now:
What would you do every day even if you weren't paid for it?

_____
_____
_____
_____
_____
_____
_____
_____
_____
_____
_____
_____
_____
_____

Mini-Lesson:
- Your passion isn't random — it's your calling.
- Your work should reflect your gifts, not just your need for income.

Activity:
Dream Career Map:
- List your top 3 dream careers.
- Identify one step you can take toward each today.

Critical Thinking Questions:
1. Why is it important to dream beyond survival and into purpose?

_____
_____
_____
_____
_____
_____
_____

2. How do your passions give clues about your destiny?

_____
_____
_____
_____
_____
_____
_____
_____
_____
_____
_____
_____

Journal Prompt:
Describe your dream career and what it would allow you to give back to your community.
[Write two full paragraphs.]

_____
_____
_____
_____
_____
_____
_____
_____
_____
_____
_____
_____
_____
_____
_____
_____
_____
_____

Lesson 2: Career Day Panel Preparation and Event

Objective:
Students will prepare to network and learn from professionals by engaging in a Career Day Panel.

Do Now:
If you could ask a professional any question about success, what would it be?

_____
_____
_____
_____
_____

Mini-Lesson:
- Exposure to success expands your possibilities.
- Learning from real-world experiences accelerates your growth.

Activity:
Career Day Prep:
- Brainstorm 5 questions to ask professionals at Career Day.
- Reflect on which fields you want to learn more about.

Critical Thinking Questions:
1. How does connecting with professionals help you build your own success path?

_____
_____
_____
_____
_____
_____
_____
_____
_____
_____
_____
_____
_____
_____
_____

2. Why is mentorship and networking crucial at every stage of growth?

_____
_____
_____
_____
_____
_____
_____
_____
_____
_____
_____
_____
_____

Journal Prompt:
After Career Day, what was your biggest takeaway about achieving success?
[Write two full paragraphs.]

_____
_____
_____
_____
_____
_____
_____
_____
_____
_____
_____
_____
_____
_____
_____
_____

Lesson 3: Resume Workshop

Objective:
Students will learn the basics of creating a professional resume that highlights their skills, experiences, and aspirations.

Do Now:
What skill, activity, or experience are you most proud of so far?

_____
_____
_____
_____
_____
_____

Mini-Lesson:
- Your resume is your personal marketing tool.
- Highlight not just jobs, but leadership, service, skills, and passions.

Activity:
Resume Builder:
- Draft your first resume or update your current one with guidance.

Critical Thinking Questions:
1. Why is it important to start building your resume even while you're young?

_____
_____
_____
_____
_____
_____
_____
_____
_____
_____
_____
_____
_____
_____

2. How does showcasing your experiences prepare you for future opportunities?

_____
_____
_____
_____
_____
_____
_____
_____
_____
_____
_____
_____
_____

Journal Prompt:
If someone only had your resume to understand your dreams and ambition, what story would it tell?
[Write two full paragraphs.]

_____
_____
_____
_____
_____
_____
_____
_____
_____
_____
_____
_____
_____
_____
_____
_____

Lesson 4: Short Term Goals

Objective:
Students will understand how to set and achieve short-term goals to build momentum toward long-term dreams.

Do Now:
Name one goal you would like to accomplish within the next 30 days.

_____
_____
_____
_____
_____
_____

Mini-Lesson:
- Success is a staircase, not a rocket ship.
- Small wins stack into big victories.

Activity:
Short-Term Goal Builder:
- Write down one short-term goal and break it into 3 action steps.

Critical Thinking Questions:
1. Why are short-term goals crucial for maintaining motivation?

_____
_____
_____
_____
_____
_____
_____

2. How does focusing on daily progress help you master your future?

_____
_____
_____
_____
_____
_____
_____
_____

Journal Prompt:

What short-term goal will you complete this month and how will you stay focused?
[Write two full paragraphs.]

_____
_____
_____
_____
_____
_____
_____
_____
_____
_____
_____
_____
_____
_____
_____
_____
_____
_____
_____
_____
_____

Lesson 5: Long Term Goals

Objective:
Students will craft long-term goals and visualize the life they want to build over the next 5-10 years.

Do Now:
Imagine your life in 10 years. What do you see?

_____
_____
_____
_____
_____
_____
_____
_____
_____
_____

Mini-Lesson:
- Vision without action is fantasy. Vision with action is destiny.
- Long-term thinking protects you from short-term distractions.

Activity:
Legacy Goals:
- Draft your 5-year and 10-year vision plans.

Critical Thinking Questions:
1. Why is it important to think beyond today when setting your goals?

_____
_____
_____
_____
_____
_____
_____
_____
_____

2. How does a clear long-term vision give you strength in hard times?

_____

_____

_____

_____

_____

_____

_____

_____

Journal Prompt:
What is one major goal you will commit to achieving in the next 5 years?
[Write two full paragraphs.]

_____

_____

_____

_____

_____

_____

_____

_____

_____

_____

_____

_____

_____

_____

_____

_____

_____

Lesson 6: Financial Literacy

Objective:
Students will learn the basics of financial literacy to build economic independence and legacy.

Do Now:
What's one thing you would like to understand better about money?

_____
_____
_____
_____
_____
_____
_____
_____
_____

Mini-Lesson:
- Wealth is not just money — it's knowledge, discipline, and freedom.
- Financial independence starts with financial intelligence.

Activity:
Money Moves:
- List 5 habits of financially successful people.
- Identify one financial habit you will start practicing today.

Critical Thinking Questions:
1. How does financial literacy protect your freedom and future?

_____
_____
_____
_____
_____
_____
_____
_____

2. Why is wealth-building a revolutionary act for our community?

_____
_____
_____
_____
_____
_____
_____
_____

Journal Prompt:
What financial goals do you have, and how will you begin building toward them?
[Write two full paragraphs.]

_____
_____
_____
_____
_____
_____
_____
_____
_____
_____
_____
_____
_____
_____
_____
_____
_____
_____
_____

Lesson 7: Building Wealth and Generational Legacy

Objective:
Students will understand how to shift from personal success to creating wealth that impacts generations.

Do Now:
If you had the power to change your family's financial future, what would you do?

_____
_____
_____
_____
_____
_____
_____
_____
_____

Mini-Lesson:
- True wealth is about legacy, not just luxury.
- Build something your great-grandchildren can thank you for.

Activity:
Legacy Blueprint:
- Design a basic plan for a wealth-building path (education, entrepreneurship, investing, giving).

Critical Thinking Questions:
1. Why is building generational wealth a form of revolutionary love?

_____
_____
_____
_____
_____
_____
_____
_____
_____
_____

2. How can your daily choices today impact people you will never meet?

_____

_____

_____

_____

_____

_____

_____

Journal Prompt:
What is the legacy you want to leave financially, socially, and spiritually?
[Write two full paragraphs.]

_____

_____

_____

_____

_____

_____

_____

_____

_____

_____

_____

_____

_____

_____

_____

_____

_____

_____

_____

_____

Knowledge of SELF (Social Empowerment Learning Framework)

Young Adult Edition (Ages 18–21) — Student Workbook

Unit Five: Good People Skills

Lesson 1: Conflict Resolution

Objective:
Students will understand effective conflict resolution strategies to maintain peace, dignity, and leadership.

Do Now:
Think of a time when you successfully resolved a conflict. What worked?

_____
_____
_____
_____
_____
_____
_____

Mini-Lesson:
- Conflict is inevitable — drama is optional.
- Resolution is about clarity, not always agreement.

Activity:
Resolution Scripts:
- Write 2–3 ways you could peacefully resolve a disagreement with respect and strength.

Critical Thinking Questions:
1. Why is emotional intelligence critical in conflict resolution?

_____
_____
_____
_____
_____
_____
_____
_____

2. How does managing conflict wisely earn you respect as a leader?

_____
_____
_____
_____
_____
_____
_____

Journal Prompt:
Describe how you can become a peacemaker without becoming a pushover.
[Write two full paragraphs.]

_____
_____
_____
_____
_____
_____
_____
_____
_____
_____
_____
_____
_____
_____
_____
_____
_____
_____
_____
_____
_____

Lesson 2: Group Cooperation

Objective:
Students will learn how to effectively collaborate, honor diverse strengths, and lead within teams.

Do Now:
Describe a time when you worked successfully with a team. What made it work?

_____
_____
_____
_____
_____
_____
_____
_____

Mini-Lesson:
- Cooperation doesn't mean losing your voice — it means adding your voice to build something greater.
- Every great vision requires a great team.

Activity:
Teamwork Practice:
- Participate in a small group challenge to practice cooperation and leadership.

Critical Thinking Questions:
1. Why is cooperation essential for community building?

_____
_____
_____
_____
_____
_____
_____
_____
_____

2. How does learning to lead and follow create stronger teams?

_____

_____

_____

_____

_____

_____

_____

_____

Journal Prompt:
What role do you naturally take in groups? Leader, supporter, strategist? Why?
[Write two full paragraphs.]

_____

_____

_____

_____

_____

_____

_____

_____

_____

_____

_____

_____

_____

_____

_____

_____

Lesson 3: Friendship

Objective:
Students will define healthy friendship traits and understand how to build meaningful, lasting connections.

Do Now:
What's one trait you value most in a friend?

_____
_____
_____
_____
_____
_____
_____
_____

Mini-Lesson:
- Real friends sharpen you, not diminish you.
- Friendship is a mirror of how you see yourself.

Activity:
Friendship Standards:
- List 5 non-negotiables you require in a true friendship.

Critical Thinking Questions:
1. Why must you be the kind of friend you want to attract?

_____
_____
_____
_____
_____
_____
_____
_____
_____

2. How does who you surround yourself with shape your destiny?

_____
_____
_____
_____
_____
_____
_____
_____
_____

Journal Prompt:
What kind of friendships will you nurture to support your purpose and peace?
[Write two full paragraphs.]

_____
_____
_____
_____
_____
_____
_____
_____
_____
_____
_____
_____
_____
_____
_____
_____
_____
_____
_____
_____
_____
_____

Lesson 4: Identifying Unhealthy Relationships

Objective:
Students will recognize the signs of unhealthy relationships and learn strategies for maintaining boundaries.

Do Now:
Think of a relationship (friendship, family, or romantic) that helped you grow. What made it healthy?

_____

_____

_____

_____

_____

_____

_____

_____

_____

Mini-Lesson:
- Unhealthy relationships drain; healthy ones build.
- Love yourself enough to walk away from what dims your light.

Activity:
Relationship Health Check:
- Create a two-column chart: Healthy vs. Unhealthy Relationship Traits.

Critical Thinking Questions:
1. Why is it important to recognize unhealthy patterns early?

_____

_____

_____

_____

_____

_____

_____

_____

_____

2. How does protecting your peace also protect your purpose?

_____
_____
_____
_____
_____
_____
_____
_____

Journal Prompt:
Describe how you will honor your peace when faced with toxic energy.
[Write two full paragraphs.]

_____
_____
_____
_____
_____
_____
_____
_____
_____
_____
_____
_____
_____
_____
_____
_____
_____

Lesson 5: Self-Love

Objective:
Students will develop a deeper understanding of self-love as the foundation for all healthy relationships.

Do Now:
What does self-love look like to you in action?

_____
_____
_____
_____
_____
_____
_____
_____
_____

Mini-Lesson:
- Self-love is not arrogance — it's necessary survival.
- How you treat yourself sets the tone for how others treat you.

Activity:
Self-Love Contract:
- Write a personal commitment letter to honor and protect your self-worth.

Critical Thinking Questions:
1. How does self-love change the way you allow others to treat you?

_____
_____
_____
_____
_____
_____
_____
_____
_____
_____

2. Why is building your self-esteem the ultimate act of revolution?

_____
_____
_____
_____
_____
_____
_____
_____

Journal Prompt:
Write your personal affirmation of self-love and protection.
[Write two full paragraphs.]

_____
_____
_____
_____
_____
_____
_____
_____
_____
_____
_____
_____
_____
_____
_____

Lesson 6: Communication Skills

Objective:
Students will master the basics of assertive, respectful communication to build stronger connections.

Do Now:
What's one quality that makes someone a great communicator?

_____
_____
_____
_____
_____
_____
_____
_____

TM

Mini-Lesson:
- Communication is the bridge between isolation and connection.
- Listen to understand, not just to respond.

Activity:
Effective Dialogue Practice:
- Pair up for a communication exercise focusing on listening and clarity.

Critical Thinking Questions:
1. How does clear communication help prevent conflicts?

_____
_____
_____
_____
_____
_____
_____
_____
_____

2. Why is listening just as important as speaking?

_____
_____
_____
_____
_____
_____
_____
_____

Journal Prompt:
Describe a time when good communication made a situation better.
[Write two full paragraphs.]

_____
_____
_____
_____
_____
_____
_____
_____
_____
_____
_____
_____
_____
_____

Lesson 7: Emotional Intelligence

Objective:
Students will explore emotional intelligence as the key to mastering relationships, leadership, and personal peace.

Do Now:
Why is it powerful to understand your own emotions?

_____
_____
_____
_____
_____
_____
_____
_____
_____

Mini-Lesson:
- Emotional intelligence (EQ) often outweighs IQ in success.
- Mastering your emotions is mastering your power.

Activity:
EQ Self-Assessment:
- Reflect on your emotional triggers and create strategies for emotional growth.

Critical Thinking Questions:
1. How does emotional intelligence strengthen leadership and teamwork?

_____
_____
_____
_____
_____
_____
_____
_____
_____
_____

2. Why must you master yourself before leading others?

_____
_____
_____
_____
_____
_____
_____
_____

Journal Prompt:
How will increasing your emotional intelligence help you navigate life better?
[Write two full paragraphs.]

_____
_____
_____
_____
_____
_____
_____
_____
_____
_____
_____
_____
_____
_____
_____

Post-Reflection Survey

After completing the Knowledge of SELF curriculum, reflect on the following:

1. What is something new you learned about yourself?

2. How has your definition of success changed?

3. What parts of your identity do you embrace more now than before?

4. What are three personal goals you now feel ready to achieve?

5. How will you use what you've learned to uplift others?

TM